Nations of the
Eastern
Great Lakes

Rebecca Sjonger & Bobbie Kalman

Crabtree Publishing Company

www.crabtreebooks.com

Nations of the Eastern Great Lakes

Created by Bobbie Kalman

Dedicated by Samantha Crabtree
To Nahtoyha, my beautiful little native princess

Editor-in-Chief
Bobbie Kalman

Writing team
Rebecca Sjonger
Bobbie Kalman
Kathryn Smithyman

Substantive editors
Amanda Bishop
Deanna Brady

Editors
Molly Aloian
Kristina Lundblad
Kelley MacAulay

Art director
Robert MacGregor

Design
Katherine Kantor

Production coordinator
Katherine Kantor

Photo research
Crystal Foxton

Consultants
Dr. Jon Parmenter, Department of History, Cornell University
Peter Cook, Assistant professor; Department of History,
    Nipissing University

Photographs and reproductions
The Granger Collection, New York: page 26 (top)
Historical Artist Robert Griffing and Publisher, Paramount Press Inc.:
    pages 8 (top), 9 (bottom), 27, 28, 29 (top), 30
Jack Paluh Arts, www.jackpaluh.com,1-814-796-4400:
    back cover (native men in canoe), page 24
© John Fadden: title page (except background)
© Permission of Lazare & Parker: front cover, pages 5, 7, 13, 15, 16 (top),
    17, 22, 23, 25 (top)
© Permission of Lewis Parker: pages 6, 18-19
Detail of painting by Ernest Smith, Rochester Museum & Science Center,
    Rochester, NY: pages 8 (bottom), 14, 20-21
Nativestock.com: page 31
"The Huron" by David Wright: page 12 (left)
Other images by Digital Stock

Illustrations
Barbara Bedell: pages 10-11, 21, 25 (snowshoe and canoe)
Katherine Kantor: border, pages 4 (map of Great Lakes), 9 (top), 11 (top),
    12 (right), 29 (bottom)
Margaret Amy Reiach: back cover (hide background),
    title page (background), 16 (bottom), 26 (bottom)
Bonna Rouse: pages 4 (map of North America), 19

Crabtree Publishing Company

www.crabtreebooks.com   1-800-387-7650

Cataloging-in-Publication Data
Sjonger, Rebecca.
  Nations of the eastern Great Lakes / Rebecca Sjonger & Bobbie
Kalman.
      p. cm. -- (Native nations of North America series)
  Includes index.
  ISBN 0-7787-0381-9 (RLB) -- ISBN 0-7787-0473-4 (pbk.)
  1. Indians of North America--Great Lakes--History. 2. Indians of
North America--Great Lakes--Social life and customs. I. Kalman,
Bobbie. II. Title. III. Native nations of North America.
  E78.G7S483 2005
  971.3004'97--dc22
                                                    2004011122
                                                          LC

**Published in
the United States**
PMB16A
350 Fifth Ave.
Suite 3308
New York, NY
10118

**Published
in Canada**
616 Welland Ave.,
St. Catharines, Ontario
Canada
L2M 5V6

**Published in the
United Kingdom**
73 Lime Walk
Headington
Oxford
OX3 7AD
United Kingdom

**Published
in Australia**
386 Mt. Alexander Rd.,
Ascot Vale (Melbourne)
VIC 3032

Contents

The eastern Great Lakes region

The Great Lakes are five huge lakes located in the northeastern part of North America. The lakes are called Lake Ontario, Lake Erie, Lake Huron, Lake Michigan, and Lake Superior. The area around Lake Ontario, Lake Erie, and to the east of Lake Huron is known as the eastern Great Lakes region. **Indigenous**, or Native, people have lived in this region for more than 12,000 years. The people belonged to various **nations**. Nations are groups of people who share languages, beliefs, customs, and leaders. The nations described in this book lived in the region during the late 1500s and early 1600s. The people of each nation lived in permanent villages, but they also hunted, fished, and gathered food throughout their **territories**.

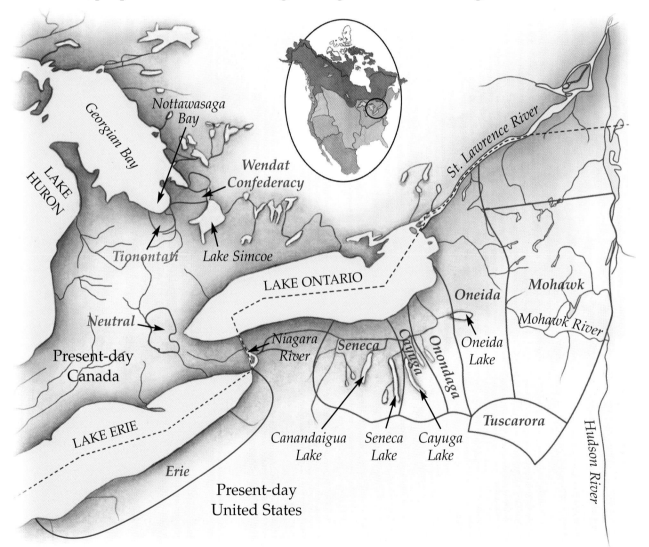

*The eastern Great Lakes region includes many lakes and rivers. The region was once covered in dense forests that were home to many plants and animals. The lakes and forests provided food and **resources** to the Native people living there. The people valued both their territories and the resources within them.*

Two confederacies

Most of the eastern Great Lakes nations belonged to one of two **confederacies**. A confederacy is an association of two or more nations that join together to achieve common goals. The nations in each confederacy worked together to establish peaceful relationships. The **Haudenosaunee Confederacy** included the people of the Mohawk, Seneca, Onondaga, Oneida, and Cayuga nations. The **Wendat Confederacy** was made up of the Attignaouantan, Attigneenongnahac, Arendahronon, and Tohontaenrat nations.

Iroquoian languages

The people of each nation spoke a different language. All the languages spoken by people of the Haudenosaunee and Wendat confederacies belonged to the Iroquoian **language family**. A language family is made up of languages that are similar to one another. Nations that lived close to one another spoke languages that were more similar than the languages spoken by nations that lived far apart.

The people of the two confederacies led similar lifestyles because they relied on the same materials from nature to survive.

5

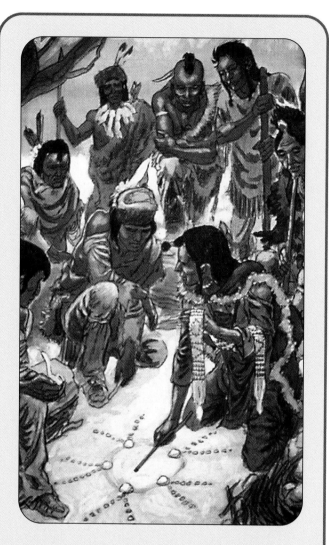

The Haudenosaunee Confederacy

Early in their history, the Mohawk, Seneca, Onondaga, Oneida, and Cayuga people often fought with one another. Haudenosaunee **oral tradition** explains that a man called the Peacemaker had a vision of unity among the nations. He shared his plans for peace with a man named Hiawatha. Together, they traveled from village to village, visiting all five nations. The pair convinced the **chiefs**, or leaders, of each nation to follow a set of laws that encouraged them to work toward common goals.

Joining together

By 1570, the five nations formed the Haudenosaunee Confederacy. Over time, the leaders of each nation met and formed the Haudenosaunee **grand council**. The members of the grand council made decisions for the entire confederacy. European settlers called the confederacy the League of Five Nations or the League of the Iroquois. In 1722, a sixth nation joined the confederacy. The Oneidas invited the Tuscaroras, who had once lived on Oneida lands and who spoke a similar language to the Oneidas, to move from present-day North Carolina into the eastern Great Lakes region. The confederacy then became known as the Six Nations.

People of the longhouse

The Peacemaker and Hiawatha told the people of the five nations that, since their territories were close together, they should treat one another as though they lived in the same **longhouse**. A longhouse was the traditional dwelling of the people of this region. To live peacefully, the people in a longhouse had to cooperate. "Haudenosaunee" means "people of the longhouse." The Mohawk, the Seneca, and the Onondaga were the "elder brothers" of the confederacy, whereas the Oneida and the Cayuga were the "younger brothers."

The grand council

The grand council was made up of 50 leaders from the five nations. They met at least once a year to discuss relations with outside nations, plan warfare, and resolve disagreements. They tried to come to **unanimous decisions**, or decisions in which every person agreed on the action to be taken. A vote was sometimes necessary to settle major decisions, such as whether or not to go to war.

Strength and power

By working together, the Haudenosaunee became the strongest and most influential group in the region. They were powerful because they did not go to war against one another. For example, if the Mohawks decided to go to war and their decision was supported by the grand council, the Mohawks could be sure that the nations from within the confederacy would never join with the Mohawks' enemies.

Although all the leaders in the Haudenosaunee grand council were men, it was the women who selected the leaders who spoke on behalf of their nations.

Although they were part of a confederacy, the people of each eastern Great Lakes nation lived according to their own traditions and beliefs. The Mohawks, the Senecas, and the Onondagas were known as the elder brothers of the Haudenosaunee Confederacy because their territories were located in areas that represented important parts of a longhouse.

The Mohawks

The Mohawks controlled the easternmost part of the region—they lived in the Mohawk River Valley in present-day New York. In the early 1600s, about 7,740 members of the Mohawk nation lived in this area. Within the confederacy, Mohawks were known as "the keepers of the eastern door." It was their duty to protect the five nations from any trouble that came from the east.

Kanienkehaka

The Mohawk people chipped **flint** from the earth. Flint is a type of rock found in traditional Mohawk territory. The people were experts at shaping flint into arrowheads, knives, and other tools. They called themselves "Kanienkehaka" which means "people of the land of flint."

The Senecas

The Seneca people called themselves "Onotowaka" or "people of the big hill." According to oral tradition, the first Senecas came into the world from beneath a large hill on Canandaigua Lake, known as "Ge-nun-de-wah" or "great hill." The Senecas lived in the western part of the eastern Great Lakes region, between the southwestern shores of Lake Ontario and the western tip of Lake Erie. In the early 1600s, the Seneca nation had about 4,000 members. They were known as "the keepers of the western door" within the confederacy. It was their duty to protect the five nations from danger from the west.

The Onondagas

The word "Onondaga" comes from the Iroquoian word "Onndagaono," which means "people of the hills." The Onondaga people lived between the Mohawks and the Senecas near Onondaga Lake in present-day central New York. In the early 1600s, there were about 4,000 Onondaga people living in this area. The Onondaga territory was smaller than the Mohawk or Seneca territories, but the Onondaga still lived in large villages. They were known as the "firekeepers." Grand council meetings took place in their territory.

Like many Haudenosaunee people, the Senecas tattooed their bodies. These Seneca warriors also painted their faces to express their personalities and to fill their enemies with fear.

9

The younger brothers

The Oneidas and the Cayugas, along with the Onondagas, lived between the territories of the Mohawks and the Senecas. Oneida and Cayuga territories were located south of Lake Ontario in present-day New York state. Their position as younger brothers within the confederacy did not mean these nations were less important than the other nations.

At grand council, the chiefs from the Oneida and Cayuga nations had equal power. Like all council chiefs, they made decisions that would benefit the daily lives of their people.

Oneida women were highly respected by the people of their nations. The survival of the people depended on work done by women, such as gathering foods, making clothes, and caring for children.

The Oneidas

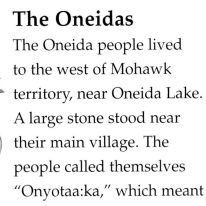

The Oneida people lived to the west of Mohawk territory, near Oneida Lake. A large stone stood near their main village. The people called themselves "Onyotaa:ka," which meant "people of the standing stone." In the early 1600s, there were about 2,000 Oneidas living in the eastern Great Lakes region.

The Cayugas

The people of the Cayuga nation lived west of Onondaga territory and east of Seneca territory, near Cayuga Lake. The territory was much smaller than the lands of the surrounding nations. Despite their smaller territory, nearly 4,000 Cayugas lived in three main villages in the early 1600s.

The Wendat Confederacy

The Wendat Confederacy was made up of four nations—the Attignaouantan, the Attigneenongnahac, the Tohontaenrat, and the Arendahronon. "Wendat" means "people of the island." The traditional territories of these people were almost completely surrounded by lakes and rivers. The territories were located between Georgian Bay and Lake Simcoe in present-day Ontario, Canada. The people traveled long distances around the Great Lakes and on the St. Lawrence River, trading items such as corn and tobacco with neighboring nations.

Who are the Huron?
Some Wendat men wore **roaches**, which were spiky hairpieces made from deer hair. When French explorers first saw the Wendat in the 1600s, they thought the roaches looked like the hair of wild boars. The French word *hure* describes a boar, which is why the French called the people of the Wendat confederacy "Huron." Other Europeans also used the name Huron and called the Wendat territory Huronia.

Confederate nations

The Wendat Confederacy began possibly as early as 1400, when the Attignaouantan and Attigneenongnahac nations formed an **alliance**, or partnership. The alliance was created mainly to prevent wars between the two nations. Many years later, after the Haudenosaunee Confederacy was formed, the Arendahronon and the Tohontaenrat were forced to move west. The Arendahronon were welcomed into the Wendat Confederacy in 1560, and the Tohontaenrat joined in 1570.

The Wendat council

Chiefs from each nation in the Wendat Confederacy joined together regularly for councils. The purpose of the council meetings was to resolve any disputes between the nations and to make decisions on issues that were important to the nations as a group. The main issues were peace, war, and trade with other nations. The people of each nation retained control over their own territory and followed their own traditions in their day-to-day lives.

The Wendat nations were friendly with one another and with the Algonquin people to the north. Above, a Wendat and an Algonquin chief participate in a tobacco ceremony before discussing trade.

Eries, Neutrals, and the Tionontati

Other nations and confederacies of nations also lived in the eastern Great Lakes region. The Eries, the Neutrals, and the Tionontati were three groups that were **allies**, or partners, of the Wendat. They traded with one another and joined together to protect their territories from enemy attacks. When the Europeans arrived, they often mistook Erie, Neutral, or Tionontati people for members of the Wendat group because the lands of these nations were close to Wendat lands.

The Eries

The Eries were known as "nation of the cat" because there were many wild cats in their territory. The Eries lived southeast of Lake Erie in present-day New York, Pennsylvania, and Ohio. In the 1600s, about 12,000 of these people lived in the area. The Eries were skilled farmers who lived in one place all year long.

The Neutral Confederacy

The traditional names for the nations known as the Neutrals have been lost over time. The name "Neutral" refers to the decision these nations made not to choose sides in conflicts between the Wendat and the Haudenosaunee. The Neutrals lived north of Lake Erie, in present-day Canada. In the early 1600s, there were about 12,000 Neutral people. A group called the Wenro were closely linked to the Neutrals, but they lived in a territory farther south along the Niagara River.

The painting above shows Jigonsaseh, a member of the Neutral nation, telling Erie and Mohawk war parties to put down their weapons. She then guided the warriors to make peace through discussions.

The Tionontati

When seventeenth-century French explorers arrived in the Nottawasaga Bay area north of Lake Ontario, they met a group of Native people who were experts in growing tobacco crops. The French called them "Petun," which means "tobacco" in French. These people were called "Tionontati," which means "on the other side of the mountain," by the people of the Wendat nations. In the early 1600s, there were about 7,000 members in the Tionontati nation. They had a close relationship with the Wendat and would later form a new nation with various members of the confederacy (see page 28).

When the people of the region were making important agreements, they smoked tobacco in ceremonial pipes. Smoking was a way of honoring the spirits and including them in the decision.

Families and clans

People in the eastern Great Lakes region lived in large **extended families** that included grandparents, parents, children, aunts, uncles, and cousins. Young children were raised by their mothers and their mothers' **siblings**. They learned about responsibilities by watching adults. The children saw that women planted and raised crops and that men hunted animals for food. They learned that the roles of men and women were of equal value. As they grew, children were taught to respect the land and everything that came from it.

Clans

Each person also belonged to a **clan**. Clans were groups of people who believed that they shared an **ancestor**. The ancestor was represented by an animal spirit, such as a bear. Membership in a clan was **matrilineal**, which means that children belonged to their mothers' clans. Each nation had a different number of clans. For example, the Cayuga had nine clans, whereas the Tionontati had only two. Some nations shared one or more clans. The Seneca and Mohawk, for example, shared the wolf clan. Members of the same clan who were from different villages and nations thought of one another as family.

Children were taught that each person in the village was important but still needed the others who lived there.

16

Clan councils

Decisions about important clan matters were discussed at different councils. Trusted and respected clan leaders led the councils and oversaw the activities in each village. For example, war councils were held by leaders who had proven themselves as great warriors. These leaders decided when their villages and nations would go to battle. Large councils were held to discuss affairs concerning a nation or a confederacy. The decisions made by one council rarely interfered with the decisions made by another council.

Decision making

Women had authority and influence over major decisions. They decided who would represent their clans, villages, and nations at the various councils. Leadership responsibilities were handed down through the mothers' families. Each clan had a head woman who held great power, although she sought advice from other women. Together, the women chose suitable leaders from within their clans, who usually held their positions for life. The head woman could also take away a male leader's powers if he was a poor decision maker.

Although women were not always present at council meetings, they influenced council decisons about going to war. Women sometimes asked for a war so prisoners could be captured to take the place of dead relatives. If the women did not agree with a war, they refused to provide their warriors with food for the journey.

Village life

The people of the eastern Great Lakes region were **sedentary**, or lived in one place year-round. Their villages were home to as many as 2,000 people. Some nations, such as the Onondaga, had one or two main villages, where most of the members lived. Other nations, such as the Erie, had several groups of small villages. Each Erie village was home to only a few families.

The villages were made up of large houses known as longhouses. These buildings were long and rectangular. Each longhouse had room for about ten families. The people who lived together in a longhouse were usually members of the same clan. A clan symbol, such as a wolf or a bear, hung above the doorway of each longhouse.

Inside a longhouse

The inside of a longhouse was lined with wooden platforms, which were used for sleeping and storing dried foods, baskets, and animal furs. Each family had its own section of the longhouse. Fire pits for heating and cooking foods were shared by two families.

Surrounded by farms

The people living in the eastern Great Lakes region chose village sites that were near **fertile** land, forests, clean drinking water, and a river or stream for traveling from place to place. The fertile land that surrounded the villages was perfect for farming. The men created fields by **clearing** areas of the forest near their villages. They cleared land by setting **controlled burns**, or small fires that burned the trees, shrubs, and grass in a specific area. When the fields were cleared, they were ready to be farmed.

Crops grown by women

Farming helped many nations thrive. Women planted the seeds and looked after the fields. They grew three main crops—corn, beans, and squash—which they called the "three sisters." Women tended the crops during the growing season using tools made from wood, stone, and animal bones. Women were also responsible for collecting the harvests.

People lived and worked in their villages until resources in the area, such as wood and soil, were used up. They then worked together to move the entire village to a new location. Most villages moved every ten to twenty years.

Finding food

The people of the eastern Great Lakes did not rely only on farming for food. They were also skilled hunters, fishers, and gatherers who knew the many foods they could catch or gather from the forests, lakes, and rivers that surrounded their villages. Although the people lived in one place, they moved throughout their territories to hunt, fish, and gather food many times each year.

Hunting

Many types of wildlife lived in the forests that covered the region. Men hunted animals such as deer, moose, bears, wolves, and rabbits. The hunters shot some animals with bows and arrows. They also used traps to catch animals. Men avoided hunting during **mating seasons**, so animals could make babies and increase in number.

Fishing

Men fished in the many lakes and rivers of the region and caught a variety of fish, including trout, sturgeon, and pickerel, all year long. Some also caught turtles and crabs. In warm months, men used nets and harpoons to catch fish. In winter, they cut holes into the frozen surface of the water and waited patiently to spear fish that swam into view. Wendat men were particularly skilled at fishing.

Gathering

Women and girls searched the forests and fields near their homes to find wild foods. They gathered nuts, berries, and herbs. They also gathered plants to use as medicines. Each spring, families collected sap from maple trees to make maple sugar. Women used maple sugar to flavor many foods.

The people hunted or fished only the number of animals they needed for food or for trade.

Making food last

Native people made sure they had a selection of foods to last the entire year. The women **preserved** most foods, or prepared them so they would not spoil during the year. They air-dried many of the gathered foods and crops. They also dried meat and fish in the sun or smoked them over a fire. These preserved foods were stored in animal skins and in birchbark containers. They could be used in hearty stews and breads all year long.

Trading goods

The eastern Great Lakes nations traded goods with one another and also with the nations that lived outside the region. The Wendat, for example, often exchanged goods with the nations that lived in the western Great Lakes region. The Haudenosaunee traded among themselves and also with neighboring nations. Although both men and women prepared goods for trade, it was usually the men who traveled from place to place to trade goods and acquire new items.

The objects offered for trade depended on the resources available to each nation. Traders looked for goods that could not be found or made from resources near their own villages. People from the best farming areas traded crops for the meats and furs offered by skilled hunters. A trader from an area with plenty of birch trees may have exchanged a birchbark container for something made of a material such as copper, which was not available in his territory.

Trade between nations was carried out with respect. Each group benefited equally from the trades made.

Records of history

People of the eastern Great Lakes nations made belts and other items from **wampum**. Wampum were tiny beads made from shells. When strung together to make belts, the beads represented important events and told stories about the nations. The different colors and patterns of these belts held different meanings and were designed to record the histories of the people. These items, sometimes called "memory belts," had great spiritual value.

Peaceful offerings

Leaders from eastern Great Lakes nations offered wampum belts when they negotiated with leaders from other nations. Trade could not occur if two nations were at war, so wampum was often made to communicate messages about peace and trade.

European "money"

When the Europeans arrived in this region, many began using wampum as money to pay the Native people with whom they traded. Both Native people and Europeans made wampum belts to communicate when they wanted to make **treaties**. Many Europeans did not honor the promises they communicated to the Native people, however.

A Wendat trader holds items made from wampum.

Daily activities, transportation, and celebrations in the eastern Great Lakes region were greatly affected by the seasons. As the seasons and the weather changed, so did each nation's way of life.

Spring and summer

Spring and summer were the busiest seasons of the year. People spent as much time as they could farming, gathering, and trading. The long, warm days were spent collecting food and goods for the following year. Traders took advantage of good weather to visit other nations, while searching for items they needed for the upcoming year.

Autumn and winter

Autumn was spent harvesting crops and preserving foods. Men often went to war in autumn as well. Winter brought cold weather and short days, which were mostly spent indoors. Early winter was a busy time of year for hunters, however, as they followed the tracks left behind in the snow by animals. During the coldest months of winter, men repaired tools and weapons, women made clothing, and families gathered together for stories, dancing, and ceremonies.

Ceremonies

Certain times of the year were celebrated with important ceremonies. Ceremonies were held to give thanks and to seek blessings from the spirit world. During these special occasions, people participated in games, dancing, feasting, and **dream guessing**. Both the Wendat and the Haudenosaunee held major midwinter ceremonies that involved days of rituals. Other ceremonies celebrated harvests. For example, many nations celebrated the collection of maple sap in early spring, the gathering of wild fruit in early summer, and the harvesting of crops in early autumn.

Each winter, the Haudenosaunee gathered inside their longhouses to celebrate the Midwinter Ceremony.

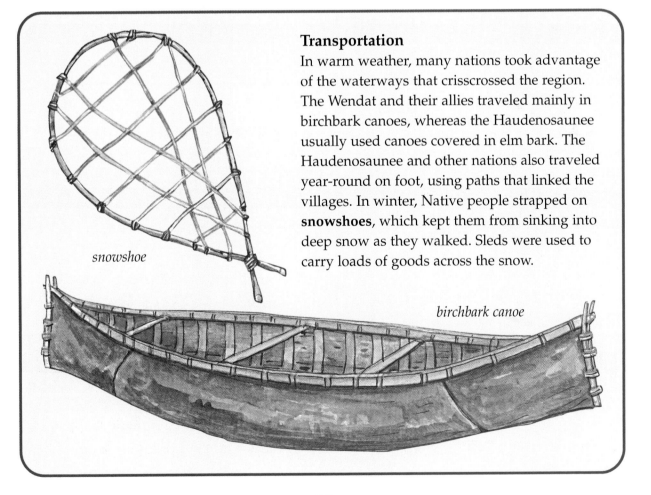

snowshoe

birchbark canoe

Transportation

In warm weather, many nations took advantage of the waterways that crisscrossed the region. The Wendat and their allies traveled mainly in birchbark canoes, whereas the Haudenosaunee usually used canoes covered in elm bark. The Haudenosaunee and other nations also traveled year-round on foot, using paths that linked the villages. In winter, Native people strapped on **snowshoes**, which kept them from sinking into deep snow as they walked. Sleds were used to carry loads of goods across the snow.

Contact with the Europeans

The Mohawks and the Arendahronon were probably the first nations in the eastern Great Lakes region to have had contact with Europeans. The Dutch arrived in Mohawk territory in 1609. French, English, and other European traders and settlers arrived in the region soon afterward. At first, the Europeans relied on Native people to show them how to survive in the wilderness. Over time, however, more settlers came looking for wealth. The greed of the Europeans eventually led to the destruction of the traditional ways of life of the nations. Fur traders recognized the skills of Native hunters and encouraged them to trap huge numbers of animals, especially beavers. In exchange for the furs, Native people were given manufactured goods such as firearms, brass kettles, and metal knives. The people of the region began using more and more of these goods instead of their traditional tools and weapons. Many traders also offered Native people alcohol as gifts or in exchange for furs. Some Native people became dependent on alcohol. Europeans sometimes encouraged Native people who were dependent on alcohol to trade away their livelihoods.

*Beaver **pelts** were sold for huge profits in Europe, where they were made into hats.*

Diseases

Many European traders and settlers carried diseases, including smallpox, measles, and typhus. Native people had not been exposed to these diseases and did not have natural defenses against them. Thousands of Native people became sick soon after they came in contact with Europeans and their goods. The diseases spread as Native people traveled from village to village to trade or to meet at councils. By the mid 1600s, almost half the Native population had died from diseases.

Missionaries

Soon after trade was established between European and Native traders, European **missionaries** arrived in the eastern Great Lakes region. They encourged the Native people to change their spiritual beliefs. Europeans favored the nations that accepted the new religions forced upon them. For example, French Catholic traders only gave firearms to Native people who claimed to be Catholic. The introduction of new beliefs even led to conflict among members of the same Native nation.

Although there were many problems between Native and non-Native people, there were also many peaceful meetings that took place. Certain European traders were interested in Native ways and learned from Native traders. The Native traders recognized the benefits of European goods, such as cloth. As a result of the trading, many Native people started using European goods.

Conflict and war

Many conflicts broke out in the eastern Great Lakes region a few decades after Europeans first made contact with the Native people. The desire for territory, resources, and control of the region influenced the actions of both European and Native people. In the early 1600s, the Wendat formed a partnership with the French. Together, they controlled much of the fur trade in the region.

The French supplied the Wendat with metal weapons—and later, firearms—that helped the Wendat defend themselves against the Haudenosaunee nations. In response, the Haudenosaunee acquired their own deadly firearms from Dutch settlers. When the British forced the Dutch out of their territory, some Haudenosaunee nations joined forces with the British.

Haudenosaunee attacks

The Haudenosaunee used their firearms to end the Wendat's control over the fur trade. In 1649, the Haudenosaunee attacked the Wendat and drove them out of their traditional territories. Many Wendat survivors were adopted into the Seneca and Mohawk nations. Others fled to neighboring Erie, Neutral, and Tionontati villages, but the Haudenosaunee continued to attack groups in the region. By the late 1650s, they had adopted, forced from their homes, or killed the Erie, Neutral, and Tionontati nations. Some of the Tionontati, along with the Wendat they were sheltering, moved south and formed a group known as the Wyandot.

Haudenosaunee men gained respect through war. When one warrior died, the other warriors took an enemy captive. The captured person either replaced the dead warrior within the nation or was tortured to death to help relieve the grief felt by the community.

Europeans at war

While the nations in the region fought one another, Britain and France also declared war over the fur trade and land. The Haudenosaunee nations remained neutral—they did not join forces with either the British or the French. In spite of this decision, warriors from some nations chose to fight alongside the British, whereas others fought alongside the French. The British defeated the French in 1760.

The American Revolution

Settlers in the **colonies** began to resent British rule. The resentment led to the **American Revolution** in 1775. Once again, some Native warriors chose to fight. Many nations supported the British because the new Americans posed a greater threat to their lands. The war led to conflicts within the Haudenosaunee Confederacy, when every nation except the Oneidas and the Tuscaroras joined with the British. Even before the American army defeated the British, it raided Haudenosaunee villages to weaken the nations.

A model government
Benjamin Franklin, Thomas Jefferson, and the other writers of the United States Constitution sought to create a **democracy**. A democracy is a government made up of elected leaders who make decisions for the people in a country. Some historians believe that Franklin and Jefferson studied the Haudenosaunee Confederacy before writing the United States Constitution. Alhough the Haudenosanee were recognized for their way of governing, they were not treated as equal citizens.

New ways of life

Over time, some of the Native people who lived in the eastern Great Lakes region were forced to leave their villages by the American, British—and later Canadian—governments. The governments prepared treaties that set aside land on which Native people could live. The parcels of land are known as **reservations** in the United States and **reserves** in Canada. A few nations were able to remain on parts of their original territories, but others were forced to relocate. For example, many Haudenosaunee who lived in the present-day United States were moved to the Buffalo Creek Reservation, and later, to other reservations. Some nations moved voluntarily. For example, many nations in present-day Canada willingly moved to the Six Nations Reserve.

Acceptance and awareness

American and Canadian governments attempted to force Native people to **assimilate**, or replace their own beliefs, languages, and customs with European languages and traditions. Many nations and Native organizations, however, fought for their rights and forced national governments to accept their cultures and ensure that Native people are treated fairly under the law. Native people continue to resist the pressure to assimilate by teaching their children traditional languages and cultures so that this knowledge may be passed on.

Life today

About 100,000 **descendants**, or relatives, of the original nations of the Great Lakes still live in the region today. They are members of various Iroquois and Wendat nations. Though their lifestyles are very similar to those of other Americans and Canadians, the people still celebrate their heritages. The nations continue to be governed by councils that meet to discuss issues of importance. The councils help their members by providing health and legal services and by funding education for both children and adults. Many nations operate successful businesses that employ both Native and non-Native people from the communities in their regions. The nations also work with the American and Canadian governments to deal with laws and issues that affect all Native people.

Celebrating Native culture
Many Native people are proud of their heritages. They celebrate traditional clothing, art, and ceremonies to keep their cultures alive. Ancient traditions, such as the sport of **lacrosse**, are part of the daily lives of many people through organizations such as the Iroquois Lacrosse Association. Artists celebrate their heritages by painting, carving, and making traditional items such as baskets and clothing.

Glossary

Note: Boldfaced words that are defined in the book may not appear in the glossary.

American Revolution The war between the American colonies and Great Britain (1775–1783), which led to the formation of the United States

ancestor An ancient relative or spirit animal from whom or from which someone is believed to have descended

colony An area ruled by a faraway country

descendant A person who comes from a particular ancestor or group of ancestors

dream guessing A sacred part of the Midwinter Ceremony during which Haudenosaunee people share their dreams with others who listen and interpret the dreams; also known as dream sharing

fertile Describing land that is capable of producing crops abundantly

lacrosse A game created by Native people, in which two teams of players use long-handled sticks to put a ball into the opposing team's goal

mating season The time of year during which animals produce babies

missionary A priest or other religious person who travels from place to place to convert people to a religion

oral tradition The stories that are told, from one generation to the next, about a group of people and their history

pelt The skin of an animal with the fur or hair still on it

resource An available supply of items, such as trees, which are used to make everyday items such as houses

sibling A brother or a sister

snowshoes Round or oval wooden frames with strips of leather woven across them, which are strapped to the feet and used for walking on snow

territory An area of land and water on which a group of people traditionally lived, hunted, fished, and gathered food

treaty A contract or agreement

Index

1 2 3 4 5 6 7 8 9 0 Printed in the U.S.A. 4 3 2 1 0 9 8 7 6 5